GUIDELINES

D1189552

pastor-parish relations

Connecting the Pastor, Staff, and Congregation

Betsey Heavner
General Board of Discipleship

PASTOR-PARISH RELATIONS

Copyright © 2008 by Cokesbury

This book is printed on acid-free paper.

ISBN 978-0-687-64781-1

Some paragraph numbers for and language in the Book of Discipline *may have changed in the 2008 revision, which was published after these Guidelines were printed. We regret any inconvenience.*

MANUFACTURED IN THE UNITED STATES OF AMERICA

Contents

Welcome

You are so important to the life of the Christian church! You have consented to join with other people of faith who, through the millennia, have sustained the church by extending God's love to others. You have been called and have committed your unique passions, gifts, and abilities to a position of leadership. This Guideline will help you understand the basic elements of that ministry within your own church and within The United Methodist Church.

Called to Spiritual Leadership

Each person is called to ministry by virtue of his or her baptism, and that ministry takes place in all aspects of daily life, in and outside the church. As a pastoral leader or leader among the laity, your ministry is not just a "job," but a spiritual endeavor. You *are* a spiritual leader now, and others will look to you for spiritual leadership. What does this mean?

First, *all* persons who follow Jesus are called to grow spiritually through the practice of various Christian habits (or "means of grace") such as prayer, Bible study, private and corporate worship, acts of service, Christian conferencing, and so on. Jesus taught his disciples practices of spiritual growth and leadership that you, as a disciple, are to share with others as they look to you to be a model and guide.

Second, it means that you always keep your eye on the main reasons for any ministry—to help others grow to a mature faith in God that moves them to action on behalf of others, especially "the least" (see Matthew 25:31-46). This is an aspect of "disciple making," which is the ultimate goal of all that we do in the church.

CULTIVATING VISION AND MISSION

As a spiritual leader, a primary function you carry is to help those you lead to see as clearly as possible what God is calling your church to be and to do. Ideally, your church council first forms this vision and then forms plans and goals for how to fulfill that vision. As a leader, you will help your team remain focused and accountable to honor the vision and goals to which the church is committed. You will help your team create and evaluate suggestions, plans, and activities against the measure: *Does this move us closer to our church's vision to bring others to God in this place and time?*

CHRISTIAN CONFERENCING

While there are appropriate and useful business-like practices that apply to church life, Christian practices distinguish the church as the church. In the United Methodist tradition, how we meet and work together is important. "Christian Conferencing" involves listening not only to each other, but also listening intently for the will of God in any given task or conversation. This makes prayer essential in the midst of "business as usual." As Christians, we are called to "speak the truth in love." This is a special way to speak in which we treat one another as if each of us were Christ among us. As a spiritual leader in your ministry area, you have the privilege and opportunity to teach and model these practices. By remembering that each of us is beloved of God and discerning the presence of God in all that the church does, every task becomes worshipful work.

THE MISSION OF THE UNITED METHODIST CHURCH

The United Methodist Church is a connectional church, which means in part that every local church is interrelated through the structure and organization of districts, conferences, jurisdictions, and central conferences in the larger "family" of the denomination. *The Book of Discipline of The United Methodist Church* describes, among other things, the ministry of all United Methodist Christians, the essence of servant ministry and leadership, how to organize and accomplish that ministry, and how our connectional structure works (see especially ¶¶125–138).

Our Church is more than a structure; it is a living organism. The *Discipline* describes our mission to proclaim the gospel and to welcome people into the body of Christ, to lead people to a commitment to God through Jesus Christ, to nurture them in Christian living by various means of grace, and to send persons into the world as agents of Jesus Christ (¶122). Thus, through you—and many other Christians—this very relational mission continues.

(For help in addition to this Guideline and the *Book of Discipline*, see "Resources" at the end of your Guideline, www.umc.org, and the other websites listed on the inside back cover.)

The Staff/Pastor-Parish Relations Committee

t he Staff/Pastor-Parish Relations Committee is the administrative unit in a local church where staff and congregational interests come together to focus on the mission of the church. Every congregation must have a S/PPRC to build relationships among members of the congregation and the staff that are most effective for accomplishing the mission and purpose of the church. Historically, the church is most effective when leaders who are growing in faith come together for a common purpose. During times of church growth and revival, spiritual leaders—both lay and clergy—have served together as servants of God. You have been elected to the S/PPRC to help make God's will be done and kingdom come, as we pray in the Lord's Prayer.

Clarifying Terms

The "pastor-parish relations committee (PPRC)" is truly a staff-parish relations committee (SPRC) because the committee relates to all staff, both bishop-appointed staff and employed staff. The *Book of Discipline* uses both names for this committee to reflect the use of both terms within the various congregations of The United Methodist Church. Throughout this Guideline, we will use S/PPRC to include both forms of common usage.

The S/PPRC has both leadership and management functions in the congregation. Leadership is the role of "keeping an eye on the big picture." Even in the midst of meetings or crises, the S/PPRC members must never forget they are part of the body of Christ, and they must always be aware of the mission of God's Church. Management is the role of tending to daily activities so that details are taken care of and strategies are implemented. In other organizations, management functions may be taken care of by a personnel office or Human Resources department. There are some legal and risk management issues for which the S/PPRC has responsibility. The S/PPRC operates under God's leadership to bring together staff and congregational interests, which includes dealing with both the celebrations and disappointments inherent in any human family and church.

The S/PPRC has primary responsibility to work with staff so that the mission of the church is realized. The S/PPRC should have a clear understanding of your local church's mission and vision, built upon the mission of the wider Church. Clear understanding of your church and prayerful listening to God's direction will guide both the development of job descriptions and the assessment of staff.

The S/PPRC works with individuals and groups, including:
- the lead pastor
- all ordained leaders—both elders and deacons—appointed by the bishop
- the lay staff, full time and part time
- the congregation (individually and corporately)
- candidates for licensed and ordained ministry
- the community outside the walls of your building
- the district superintendent
- the United Methodist conference staff and general church staff.

Remember that The United Methodist Church has an appointive system rather than a call system for clergy leadership. The S/PPRC consults with the district superintendent about congregational needs. The S/PPRC members must spend time in prayer and Bible study in order to interpret the movement of God's Spirit in this consultation process among the district superintendent, staff, and congregation. Read more about the appointive system and consultation on pages 28–29.

Specific tasks for the S/PPRC are listed in the *Book of Discipline* and are summarized here.

- Educating and reminding both the staff and the congregation to focus on working together toward the mission of the church by promoting unity and encouraging, strengthening, nurturing, supporting, and respecting the pastor(s), staff, and their families.
- Leading conversation between the congregation and the staff/pastor about ministry direction, including recommendations about staff positions to carry out the work of the church.
- Developing and recommending written policy and procedures on employment of nonappointed staff, including provision for insurance, pension, and severance pay. (See the resource list for a sample policy.)
- Assessing job performance of the staff/pastor at least annually for the purpose of realigning staff position descriptions with the mission of the church.
- Conferring and consulting with the district superintendent.
- Supporting lifelong learning and spiritual renewal for all staff (continuing education).
- Identifying and supporting individuals from the congregation whom God seems to be calling for ordained ministry.

The Job of the Chairperson

Your leadership is a partnership with other congregational lay and staff leaders to discern God's direction for the focus of your ministry. In these conversations, you bring your knowledge of the gifts and skills of the staff. You represent the staff vision and dreams for church ministry and the conversations of the S/PPRC committee related to staffing and direction. You listen to the conversations for implications about staffing and refocusing job descriptions and bring reports of these leadership conversations to the S/PPRC committee meetings for strategic planning and management decisions.

- Ask God to increase your understanding of the way your skills will be used as chairperson of the staff/pastor-parish relations committee. Pray together for your congregation and the leadership each of you has.
- Read this Guideline and the current Disciplinary sections to understand the responsibility of the S/PPRC and the committee's relationships with other parts of the church system.
- Make an appointment with your pastor(s) and district superintendent to talk about expectations for the S/PPRC. The goal is to build a partnership for working together.
- Meet with the previous chairperson to learn how the committee worked in the past and how to handle any unfinished business. Get copies of job descriptions, policies, and procedures that have guided the committee.

CLARIFYING TERMS

The *Book of Discipline* describes the form of organization and governance of The United Methodist Church. It is revised according to the decisions of each General Conference, which meets every four years. The *Discipline* is organized primarily by paragraph rather than page, chapter, or section. The paragraphs are numbered consecutively within each chapter or section, but numbers may be skipped between sections to allow for future additions. There is a table of contents and a topical index. The paragraphs in the 200 section relate to the local church; the 300 section relates to the ministry of the ordained.

- Consult with chairpersons of other committees who relate to staff people. For example, trustees relate to the work of a custodian; the worship committee relates to musicians and worship leaders; the education committee relates to the director of Christian education, director of youth ministry, and daycare teachers. The S/PPRC has responsibility for proper screening, including contacting references and performing background checks on lay employees of the congregation. The S/PPRC should make sure that appropriate groups conduct background checks for volunteer staff, such as children and youth workers (see the resource *Safe Sanctuaries* for guidance).

- Develop a calendar of meetings in consultation with the pastor, other people who will attend, and the church calendar.
- Arrange for or lead training for the committee, especially new members.

HELP FOR THE JOB

People who can help you are the district superintendent; annual conference program staff people; ordained and lay leaders in your church; and people in the community outside your church who are skilled in communication, mediation and peacemaking, law, benefit programs, and social needs. Other sources of help are your annual conference board of ordained ministry, the General Board of Discipleship, the General Council on Finance and Administration, and the General Board of Higher Education and Ministry. See the Resources suggested at the back of this Guideline.

A CHECKLIST FOR CONVERSATION WITH PASTOR AND DISTRICT SUPERINTENDENT

_____ What are conference parsonage standards?

_____ What are conference requirements for continuing education and spiritual formation?

_____ How does the S/PPRC recruit, nurture, and support candidates for certification and ordained ministry?

_____ What are conference policies related to sexual harassment and building safe sanctuaries for all people?

_____ What are conference policies for ministerial evaluation?

_____ What conference policies apply to lay employees?

The Job of the Committee Members

- Read the appropriate paragraphs in the *Book of Discipline* to learn what is expected of the staff/pastor-parish relations committee. See the box about using the *Discipline* ("Clarifying Terms"), page 8.
- Study this Guideline carefully to help you understand how the committee relates to the overall administration of your local church.
- When the committee has made its schedule of meetings, place these dates in your personal calendar. When you cannot attend, notify the chairperson.

REFLECTION

For as in one body we have many members, and not all the members have the same function, so we, who are many, are one body in Christ, and individually we are members one of another. We have gifts that differ according to the grace given to us (Romans 12:4-6a). What implication does this Scripture have for the S/PPRC?

Who Is on the S/PPRC?

The staff/pastor-parish relations committee members are nominated by the committee on lay leadership and elected by the charge or church conference. The S/PPRC should be the least homogenous group in the church. Each person should represent or relate to various constituencies in the church. The *Book of Discipline* provides for a rotation system to ensure continuity on the committee; it requires that at least five and not more than nine members be elected for terms of three years each, in three classes; it specifies that one member must be a young adult and that all members must be professing or associate members of the church or charge. Retiring members (those who have served three years) may not succeed themselves.

The *Discipline* also requires that a lay member of the annual conference and the lay leader be members of the S/PPRC. No employee of the church or a member of the pastor or staff member's immediate family may serve on the committee, nor may any affiliated ordained clergy persons. Only one person from an immediate family residing in the same household shall serve on the committee. S/PPRC members must be laypersons, other than the appointed staff. The S/PPRC of a charge where there is more than one church must have at least one representative from each church. The committees of charges in a cooperative parish shall meet together to consider professional leadership.

The committee is required to meet at least quarterly. It may be called to meet by the bishop, the district superintendent, the pastor, any other person accountable to the committee, or the chairperson of the committee. It may not meet without the knowledge of the pastor or the district superintendent. In addition, the committee shall meet in a closed session, and all information shared in the committee shall be confidential. When the pastor or any member of the staff who is under consideration is not present and that person's employment is to be discussed, that person must be informed prior to the meeting and immediately thereafter be brought into consultation either by the committee or the district superintendent.

An Overview of the Year

t he functions and responsibilities of the S/PPRC continue throughout the year. The following calendar highlights responsibilities for focus during a particular quarter and suggests a flow for the committee work. It is important that the committee always be attentive to God and be flexible in working with people and ministry.

First Quarter: January–March

Provide training or review for all committee members using this Guideline and suggestions in the resources section at the end. In reviewing responsibilities, be sure to include a report on the current status of candidates for certified and for ordained ministry recommended by the charge conference. The S/PPRC leads the congregation in supporting and encouraging candidates through the years of training and formation for leadership.

TIP: Assign a committee member to be in touch with candidates. Suggest to your education work area (in a large church) or to your district committee on ordained ministry that there could be an annual class on "Is God Calling You?" (See *Answering God's Call for Your Life* in Resources.)

Explore the nature and function of the church and ministry. Remember the mission and vision of your congregation. Review job descriptions and jointly negotiate priorities for pastor and staff to align the job descriptions with the needs and hopes of the congregation. Rewrite the job descriptions as necessary. Make plans to inform the congregation about staff responsibilities and inform the congregation whenever there is a change. Consult with the committee on lay leadership about leadership needed to complement the staff's skills, gifts, and assignments. See the Resources section for help with job descriptions.

TIP: Assign committee members to each staff member to build one-on-one relationships. Often it is best for the chairperson of the S/PPRC to build this relationship with the lead pastor. Joys and concerns may be shared with the committee as appropriate.

Second Quarter: April–June

Begin the assessment/evaluation of strategies of each ministry area/staff person. Increasingly, congregations find spring a good time to ask if the strategies for making disciples have resulted in new or more committed disciples. Spring is a good time to develop strategies with staff for reaching annual ministry goals. The goal of assessment is to improve the ministry of the congregation under the guidance of God. Effective assessment begins with a clear understanding between the S/PPRC and the staff members about the expectations of the staff members. While this underscores the importance of job descriptions (see first quarter tasks n page 11), effective assessment also calls for building positive relationships and strong communication skills among the people involved. Suggestions for conducting effective assessment are on several of the following pages. Assessment is most effective when it is done with the staff members. Agree on the steps for improving ministry. Decide who else, if anyone, will receive information from individual assessments and how the assessment will be interpreted by your committee. Assessment can be assigned to subcommittees who work with the pastor and staff members to complete the evaluation of their area of ministry. See the Resources list at end of this Guideline for help with assessment tools.

Arrange a parsonage tour with the parsonage family and a representative of the board of trustees for inventory, maintenance, and repair. Keep a liaison with the parsonage family to address issues before they become problems.

Review your legal responsibilities with employed and appointed staff. Legal responsibilities include church, state, and federal law for lay and clergy staff. (See Resources.)

Third Quarter: July–September

Review non-salary support for the pastor and staff, such as vacation, business expenses, housing allowance, and professional and continuing education expenses. Make recommendations to the finance committee for adjustments.

Review salary-and-benefits packages for the pastor and staff for the coming year and send recommendations to the church council or their consideration. (The S/PPRC may consult with the finance committee to establish those recommendations.)

Review continuing education and spiritual formation plans for the coming year with the pastor and staff.

Check with the conference board of ordained ministry to identify guides who can lead candidates through the Ministry Inquiry Process.

Interview candidates for ordination as deacon or elder using guidelines contained in *The Christian as Minister.* (See Resources.)

Follow up the third quarter evaluations of ministry areas and staff. As a committee, discuss whether the processes you have used lead to improvement in the church's ministry. Modify the evaluation process as needed. Review the strategies for ministry to check for staffing implications and to make sure there is an accountability system for new strategies.

Fourth Quarter: October–December

Compare vision/mission statements, charge conference goals, and job descriptions. Revise job descriptions to align with the mission and goals of the congregation in consultation with the pastor and the employed staff.

Evaluate the total work of this committee. Ask for input from the pastor and staff. Search for ways to improve. The committee and staff should agree on what to report to the congregation and to the church council.

Conducting Meetings

Your time together as a committee will have (or can have) a huge impact on the congregation, on the committee, and on individual and staff members of the church and S/PPRC. It is crucial that the meetings be conducted in an open, supportive, flexible, participative, and trustworthy manner.

Sample Meeting Agenda

Prepare by notifying/reminding committee members and staff of the meeting date, time, and place at least a week in advance; by planning the agenda, including worship relevant to the business of the meeting; and by coordinating with others who will make presentations. It may be helpful to mail the agenda and minutes prior to the meeting.

Open the meeting on time. Begin with worship to focus attention toward God. Use Scripture, music and other worship elements as you feel led to help the committee consider how congregation and the pastor/staff can work together to achieve goals for mission and ministry of the congregation. Ask God for guidance in planning and decision making. (There are Scripture suggestions related to aspects of the committee's work throughout this Guideline.)

Using Scripture in meetings. Invite the participants to listen for God's word and direction as you read the verses you have selected. Tell them you'll allow a time of silence after the Scripture reading so they can reflect on what they have heard. Ask them to be aware of any words or phrases that seem to stand out as you read slowly. After several minutes of silence, read the verses a second time. Invite people to talk in pairs about the passage. Allow time for group sharing and conclude the worship time with a prayer.

Have a time of learning and education for the committee related to its task. (See "Skills for Committee Members," page 16.)

Hear reports from liaisons to the pastor/staff. Any reports should be made after prior discussion with the staff members concerned. Staff members should have the opportunity to share recent joys or disappointments, plans that are progressing for the future, and the most pressing concerns.

Ask how the Scripture, learning, and reports provide insights for the work of the committee. What needs attention? What needs to be communicated to the congregation and/or the staff? What does the S/PPRC need to do in order to increase the ministry of the congregation?

Review the decisions and recommendations made during the meeting and clarify who is responsible for the actions.

Conclude with a brief evaluation of the meeting. How has the meeting helped to advance the mission and vision of your church? What issues have been raised for future agendas? How have committee members experienced God's love and guidance in this meeting? Spend some time in prayer.

Your First Meeting
Open your meeting with worship, seeking God's guidance. Use 1 Corinthians 12:4-13 as a scriptural basis for the committee's work.

Provide training about the job using the section of this booklet for committee members.

Study the paragraphs from the *Book of Discipline* that relate to the work of the committee and make plans to carry out those tasks and responsibilities. (See ¶258.2.)

Agree on the procedures for your decision-making and discussions. There are suggestions of procedures in *Behavioral Covenants in Congregations: A Handbook for Honoring Differences*, by Gilbert R. Rendle (see Resources).

Stress the absolute necessity for confidentiality as it relates to what goes on in the committee—not only the actions taken, but also the discussions preceding the actions. It is very important to discuss this when you are establishing how you will work together. It is very difficult to introduce this concept when there is tension over an issue. Remember that your administrative task of working with personnel is not the same as the program ministries of other committees. It is helpful to reflect on the difference between confidentiality (private matters shared in trust) and secrecy (something hidden or concealed).

Elect a vice-chairperson and a secretary.

Assess last year's committee activities. Which activities are ongoing? What needs to be added or taken away in order to fulfill the mission of the church? How can the committee work as a team to help the church accomplish its mission?

Skills for Committee Members

the sample agenda calls for attention to education and training for the committee. Among skills that are useful for the S/PPRC are teaching skills, communication skills, hospitality and celebration skills, and peacemaking and mediation skills.

Teaching Skills: Everyone Is a Minister

By virtue of our baptism, each Christian is a minister, and we minister to those around us. We may minister in the service organization we belong to or the baseball team or our family or the school or district, conference and global church gatherings. Through our connectional system and our individual baptisms, we reach out beyond our local church. Jesus told the disciples and us to "Go therefore and make disciples of all nations" (Matthew 28:19). The apostle Paul, writing to the church in Rome and to us, stated that *we are all members of the body of Christ* (Romans 12:4-8). Each of us has different gifts that God can use, and we are all ministers to God's saving grace.

The S/PPRC teaches and models this understanding of ministry to the rest of the congregation. Remember that each appointed and staff leader will have some of the skills and gifts for advancing the mission of the church. The S/PPRC has primary responsibility for working with staff so the mission of the church is realized.

The committee needs to assign tasks to those who have the skills necessary to do the task. Consider the lay members as well as the pastor(s) for these tasks. For example, you may find members who are skilled at making hospital calls and will offer a ministry to those hospitalized. When we affirm gifts of the laity and of the clergy and weave them together, we are truly ministers together.

The United Methodist Church recognizes several forms of ministry by ordaining, consecrating, certifying, licensing, and commissioning individuals. These are deacons, elders, local pastors, diaconal ministers, deaconesses, missionaries, and certified personnel. All of these people have committed themselves to specialized training for ministry. They, along with the laity in the local congregation, make up the ministry of the Church. You may not have all of these forms of ministry present in your congregation. Which do you have?

THE MINISTRY OF ALL CHRISTIANS

To prepare for teaching others, the S/PPRC can read Mark 2:1-12 and discuss "ministry." Complete the following thoughts:

1. I was ministering to someone when...
2. Someone ministered to me when...
3. The spiritual gift that I see in you (name of each committee member) is...
4. I believe God is leading me into a ministry of...
5. The support I can give others who minister is...
6. I would like this committee to help me develop my faith by...
7. Our committee's ministry is...

Communication Skills

The S/PPRC listens to many different voices. Listening and responding to the Church and community—congregation, community, pastor, staff, and people in the United Methodist connection—is a crucial skill. Some of these voices need help to say what they really want to say, and the S/PPRC may need to ask their opinions in interviews and surveys. The S/PPRC should use active listening skills to make certain different voices are clearly understood.

Body language is an important part of communicating. Be aware of gender and cultural differences in styles of communicating. We often reveal more about what we are thinking by our actions than by our voices. Be alert to what people are saying with their posture, gestures, hands, eyes, heads, arms, and legs.

Active listening requires the full attention of everyone involved. Without listening, no communication takes place. Careful listening is such a critical task for the S/PPRC and for the congregation that you might consider arranging training sessions. Give special attention to the gender and cultural differences in communication styles. Resources may be available in your community through sponsors of crisis hot lines or a school's communication department.

A CHECKLIST FOR GOOD COMMUNICATION

_____ Encourage the other person to stay in the present, the here-and-now. Acknowledge ways that past activities are a strong foundation for current ministry, but stay away from the "we used to do it" scenario.

_____ Begin statements with "I believe," "I feel," and "In my opinion." Encourage others to do the same.

_____ Ask what the other person is feeling, if appropriate. Remember that some people find discussion of feelings offensive or irrelevant. Be aware of your own feelings as well.

_____ Repeat what you hear to ensure accuracy. Ask questions for information and clarity.

_____ Build trust by finding what you can agree on, then move on to any differences.

_____ Accept; do not judge. This does not necessarily mean reaching an agreement.

_____ Suggest opportunities for in-depth conversation (at home, on a walk, at lunch, and so forth).

_____ Provide ways people can share new ideas. One congregation supplies pew racks with a card saying, "I wish our congregation would _____." People are encouraged to submit ideas by filling out a card and putting it in the offering plate.

Hospitality and Celebration Skills

The S/PPRC is the cheerleading squad for the staff of your church. Hospitality includes a pleasant environment for the staff to work in and the tools and equipment for the job. The S/PPRC leads the congregation in celebrating the work of the staff. Acknowledge specific examples of ways the staff builds the mission and vision of the church.

The United Methodist Book of Worship includes services to celebrate the appointment of clergy leaders and to say farewell to clergy leaders. It is also appropriate to recognize lay staff in worship, especially when praising God for the gifts of staff in leading the congregation. Remember that it is important to acknowledge staff members throughout the year, not only at the beginning or end of their appointment/employment and at Christmas time.

Deal With Rumors Proactively

Rumors begin when people discern a few facts or impressions and then fabricate the rest of the story. When any rumors begin to circulate, it is essential to communicate facts quickly. The way to stop rumors is to communicate openly and honestly what you can. Most importantly, develop a plan! Stick to the facts and remember your covenant of confidentiality.

The chairperson and committee members should all be clear about:
- who speaks on behalf of the congregation
- when you involve the district superintendent, bishop, or conference staff
- the annual conference plan for responding to the media
- how you handle the media.

To learn more about developing a plan, work with a public relations communicator in your church or community or contact the communicator who works for your annual conference. They will advise you on how to provide facts to the media to support your congregation and how to write an appropriate message. Remember, the quicker the facts are made known, the quicker the rumors will die.

Ministry Assessment Skills

The S/PPRC has primary responsibility for working with staff so that the congregation's mission and vision are fulfilled. This includes providing feedback to the congregation, the staff, and the district superintendent about the way staff and congregation work together. Open and clear communication increases the potential for mission and ministry to be the primary focus of the congregation. The S/PPRC has a critical role in communicating the ministry focus of the congregation to the staff and of helping the congregation understand new directions initiated by staff. Two-way communication should be ongoing; also, specific conversations must be scheduled to assess ministry. S/PPRC must participate in congregational ministry planning meetings, contributing and listening for staffing implications. The S/PPRC has responsibility for scheduling these conversations with staff. See pages 25–27 for more information on staff assessment.

Mediation Skills: Resolving Problems

Conflict is simply two different ideas in the same place at the same time. Conflict is normal in communities and families. *The important part of conflict management is bringing those conflicts into the open where they can be clarified.*

Good communication is a key for mediating conflict. Careful listening builds understanding by all the people who are involved. Once understanding is achieved, begin to work with one another to resolve the conflict. If the conflict is handled properly, a strengthened church can result. Know when to ask for outside mediation. Earlier is better! See suggestions in the Resources list.

STORY OF A CONGREGATION DEALING WITH CONFLICT

The church was in conflict about membership requirements. One of the leaders was bringing people who had different ways of living and acting. Here is the story (paraphrased from Acts 15).

Some Jews showed up from Judea insisting that in order to be saved, everyone be circumcised according to the Mosaic law. Paul, Barnabas, and a few others were dispatched to Jerusalem to take up the matter with the leaders there.

When Paul and Barnabas arrived in Jerusalem, the whole church, including the apostles and leaders, graciously received them. The travelers gave a glowing report of how God had sent them with good results to those outside the Jewish community, but the hard-line Pharisees insisted on imposing the Law of Moses on those converts they considered pagan.

At a special meeting to consider the matter, the conversation heated into a full-fledged argument until Peter stood to speak. "Friends, you well know that for some time now, God has spoken plainly to us that this good news is not just for Jews, but for everyone. I, myself, have been told directly to bring the Word of God to them. God is not fooled by our rationalizations or prejudices and has made no distinction between them and us. How can we in faith and good conscience require something of them that God does not require?"

That speech silenced the room long enough for Barnabas and Paul to tell them at length story after story of the signs and wonders that God had done through them among these "pagans." James, the leader of the Jerusalem church, was persuaded, and in an elegant testimony to their stories and to Scripture, spoke for the assembly, agreeing not to burden unnecessarily their new brothers and sisters in the faith. The council unanimously agreed to send several of their own members with Paul and Barnabas to Antioch to carry a welcoming letter of explanation to the Gentile believers.

Support for Clergy and Staff

the S/PPRC has an important role supporting the morale of the staff and providing positive, helpful feedback. Supporting the staff is more than saying, "Hello, how are you?" on Sunday morning. It is more than saying, "Thank you" when a staff member has performed a job. *Support is building relationships between people; it is getting to know one another so that you know when something is bothering the other person even when nothing is said.*

Pastors and staff need friendly advisers: people to suggest how best to handle some of the joys, concerns, and issues of the parish. This function of counsel determines, in large measure, the degree to which the shared vision can be achieved. *The S/PPRC members are chosen because they have the ability, by way of the Holy Spirit, to discern what the pastor (and staff) need, what the church needs, and how to bring these needs together for ministry.* The information and feedback of the S/PPRC is essential for developing the ministry direction of the congregation and pastor.

Financial Support and Benefits

Each year the committee needs to review salary and non-salary support for each staff member. Remember that your annual conference sets minimum salary recommendations for ordained ministers. Ask the lay member of the annual conference from your church to discuss the action taken by the conference with the committee before the committee makes compensation recommendations for the coming fiscal year.

For other staff members, assign a member of the committee to contact nearby churches of a similar size to discover their salary scale for the same services. This will help you determine equitable salary for your lay staff.

Other aspects of support for all employees include determining:
1. working conditions, including working space, office helpers (volunteers), equipment, and hours.
2. travel expenses, annual conference session attendance allowance, continuing education for both clergy and employed staff, moving expenses, and so forth.
3. fringe benefits for all employees, including Social Security, Worker's Compensation, insurance, opportunity for the pension program, and vacation allowances. Some conferences have vacation policies for clergy.

The *Book of Discipline* requires provision of adequate housing for pastors, and housing is not considered part of compensation (although there are federal tax implications). Check with your district superintendent to find out about conference policies for housing standards.

Your committee's recommendations go to the church council for its consideration. It is a courtesy to give a summary of your salary recommendations to the finance committee for their budget preparations, but the finance committee does not determine salary packages. The final recommendation to the charge conference may be as you recommended, or it may differ. If it differs, the S/PPRC has the right and the responsibility to advise the council or the charge conference of its recommendations and the reasoning behind that decision. However, the charge conference has the final decision on salary matters.

Continuing Education and Spiritual Formation

If individuals are to be effective in their ministry, they must have opportunities for continuing education to expand their knowledge and skills, and for spiritual formation to foster a growing relationship with God. Continuing education is not just for the ordained staff but for other church employees as well.

Ordained elders and deacons are required to report at charge conference on their continuing education and spiritual formation of the past year and plans for the new year. Many churches provide continuing education funds in addition to salary compensation. Many annual conferences have standards, requirements, and guidelines for continuing education. Check your annual conference journal or talk with a district superintendent for details. Talk with the clergy staff to develop a plan for meeting, or exceeding, these standards and guidelines.

If your pastor's plan calls for financial aid beyond your congregation, it may be possible to obtain it from the Ministerial Education Fund (MEF). One-fourth of this fund is retained in each annual conference and is administered by the conference board of ordained ministry for theological education, enlistment, and continuing education. The MEF is an apportioned fund. Your committee should tell the congregation about this fund and support 100 percent remittance to the MEF.

Talk with other staff people about their own continuing education. Church secretaries and building maintenance staff can benefit by taking advantage of seminars offered in your own community or nearby communities. Many annual conferences provide workshops for secretaries, Christian educators, youth ministers, and directors of music, choir directors, and organists. Professional organizations for United Methodists provide resources and workshops for musicians, educators, youth ministers, church secretaries, and church administrators.

Many areas for possible growth and learning are enumerated in the *Book of Discipline* (see ¶351). The pastor and other ordained leaders are allowed one week each year and one month during one year of each quadrennium (the four years between General Conferences) for continuing education and spiritual formation. This is not a vacation, but a time of learning that will enhance the ministry of the pastor and the congregation. Furthermore, a pastor who has held a full-time appointment for at least six years is permitted to request an educational leave of up to six months while continuing to hold an appointment. The pastor will need to have a careful discussion with the committee and the district superintendent if he or she is seeking such a plan. One part of such a plan is determining alternative pastoral leadership while the leave is in effect and the financial obligations that may go along with that leadership.

The S/PPRC in Ministry With Ordained, Appointed Staff

there are four ongoing functions for the staff/pastor-parish relations committee with ordained elders and deacons who are members of the annual conference and appointed to your church by the bishop. These four functions are interpretation, assessing effectiveness, providing feedback, and consulting with the district superintendent. Remember, it is not the job of the S/PPRC to define the mission and vision. Rather, the S/PPRC communicates and interprets to staff and congregation so that the congregation's ministry is aligned with its mission.

Interpretation

Continual communication and interpretation of the local church's mission and vision is one of the most important roles of the S/PPRC. The S/PPRC gives consistent reminders of the common aim and direction of ministry to church members, staff, and community. When the members take on this task sufficiently, growth in ministry is the natural result.

It's up to the S/PPRC to help the congregation learn about the forms of ministry in The United Methodist Church: lay ministry; licensed ministry; certified ministry; and ordained ministry, such as deacon and elder. The S/PPRC also tells the congregation about the United Methodist understanding of education and credentialing for clergy, about the Ministerial Education Fund, and about the open itinerancy of The United Methodist Church. Use the index at the back of the *Book of Discipline* to read more. The General Board of Higher Education and Ministry provides brochures, posters, videos, and staff to help you teach your congregation. Your district and conference boards of ordained ministry can also help.

Interpretation to the congregation is most effective when the S/PPRC members "walk the talk," that is, when the committee members are living the ministry vision they talk about. Regular worship attendance, church school or Bible study, and regular systematic giving are essential if members are to bring integrity to the interpretive function of this ministry. Living within the context of the mission and vision allows the members to speak as informed, faithful proponents about what God has given to the pastor and the people together.

Assessing Effectiveness and Providing Feedback

Measuring ministerial competence is essential to the continued growth and development of the ordained staff, the lay staff, and the local church. *Thus, the spiritual and theological value of assessment must not only be stressed, it must also be featured.* The staff/pastor-parish relations committee has the opportunity to encourage, develop, and improve the ministry of the church in untold ways when it measures the effectiveness of the local church and the staff. This process provides opportunity for the S/PPRC to help the staff focus on priority tasks for the mission and vision of the congregation. If the S/PPRC has a legal or ethical concern related to an appointed leader, it must consult with the district superintendent.

All assessment conversations begin with these considerations:
- the place where ministry takes place—the community, the church and its history, people and their history.
- mission/vision statements of the congregation and charge conference goals.
- tasks or job description of the staff person being assessed. Remember this is an assessment of effectiveness in doing the task. If the staff person does what was required, but it does not have the desired result, the plan fell short, not the staff person.
- performance of the individual. What kind of results does the individual obtain? What results do we desire and expect? How can we help ensure that the ministry plan will achieve the desired results?
- gifts, skills, and ability of the individual. What qualities are present, and which ones are lacking? How can we help by matching our needs with the available skills? Perhaps rewriting the job description will help.
- team-ministry approach. How can more members become team members to share the load?

Assessing the pastor(s) and the local church should be done in a context of Christian community. The purpose of appraisal is to build up the body of Christ. It is therefore to be exercised in a spirit of love and care. Committee members should realize that the growth and development of the congregation are dependent upon a loving yet earnest assessment, not only of the pastor but also of the congregation and how the church is bringing the good news effectively to your unique setting. The S/PPRC should develop a process that includes ongoing self-assessment, group assessment, feedback, recommendations for growth, and plans for implementing those recommendations.

The S/PPRC is responsible for the assessment of lay staff as well as appointed clergy. The committee functions to consider when changes are needed in the number of paid personnel. Ideally, staffing is developed within the vision/mission context of the local church and is not financially driven. The S/PPRC must be wise stewards of the congregation's resources while providing staffing for the congregation's ministry goals.

The *Book of Discipline* calls for the S/PPRC to provide assessment annually for the pastor's and staff's use in an effective, ongoing ministry and for identifying continuing education needs and plans (¶258.2g[3]). Your conference board of ordained ministry and cabinet has prepared the criteria, processes, and training for evaluation and continuing education. Check with them for their guidance.

The assessment process should be a dialogue with the individual being evaluated and the group or person making the assessment. The pastor and the staff should agree upon which method will be used for measurement. Completing these statements is a good start:
1. I (or we) have grown in this congregation because...
2. Strengths and satisfying experiences our pastor has had are...
3. Helpful things our staff people have done (or tried to do) were...
4. Areas for growth in this staff person are...
5. Our committee is showing its support by...

The content of those sessions needs to be from your own experiences and feelings—not what someone else has said. Be honest and straightforward as you share your feelings, but be tactful and diplomatic. Always begin with the strengths and elaborate on them. Remember that God gives each of us different gifts.

CONDUCTING ANNUAL ASSESSMENT OF STAFF

As was pointed out earlier, the committee needs to agree with the pastor and the staff about the time and procedures for annual assessment of ministry. Review the suggestions for assessment procedures on the committee calendar page: second quarter: April–June (page 12).

Here is one model for an assessment interview. There is additional information in the resource list at the end of this Guideline.

Start by asking staff members for a report of their accomplishments, and celebrate them.

Next, review the ministry goals set for the congregation, especially those that were set by the charge or church conference and by what the *Book of Discipline* says about the nature and function of a congregation. Then review the strategies you have previously set to reach these goals. Has the staff person done the strategies he or she agreed to do? Have the strategies been effective in reaching the ministry goals? Do the strategies for this staff person need to be continued or changed?

Help staff and congregation understand the priorities set for the pastoral work, administrative tasks, and building maintenance. How many hours are available each week for the different areas of ministry? (Number of people multiplied by hours equals total hours.) What financial resources are available for the different areas of ministry?

Assess the staff person's need for continuing education. Encourage each person to ask for help, as necessary, to accomplish the strategies set for the coming year. For instance, the church office staff may need special training to be able to use new equipment to its full potential; the S/PPRC should be prepared to help them obtain this training as continuing education. Church Christian education staff hired from within the congregation may need more formal training in Bible and theology or educational theory and application. Solicit the needs of the staff and the pastor and find ways to fill those needs.

Review with the staff the plan for division of responsibilities for the various areas of ministry. Should these responsibilities stay the same or be shifted? If a change is needed, the S/PPRC must determine who will carry the added responsibilities. Remember that both paid and volunteer staff can carry out strategies for reaching the ministry goals of the congregation.

Conclude the assessment by restating the past accomplishments, the future strategy details, changes in position description, and the steps you have agreed on. Pray for the staff person and the mission of your congregation.

Consulting With the District Superintendent

The United Methodist Church operates with an appointment system, unlike some other denominations in which congregations "call" a pastor. Our system of annual appointments of pastoral leaders connects all United Methodist congregations with a pool of ordained and commissioned individuals who have a wide variety of gifts and graces for leadership.

All the pastoral leaders and congregations are reviewed annually by the bishop and cabinet to match each pastor's gifts with congregational mission. Ideally, this system allows both pastors and congregations to thrive in the mission of making disciples of Jesus Christ for the transformation of the world. This is described in the *Book of Discipline,* ¶¶432–433.

This cooperative system allows United Methodists to retain qualified pastoral leaders for local churches on a continual basis. The S/PPRC is responsible for modeling and ensuring fairness, justice, and appreciation for those who facilitate God's work in the name of the church. The S/PPRC plays a vital role, along with district superintendents, bishops, and pastors in this appointive process. The S/PPRC represents the voice of the congregation.

The S/PPRC helps keep the present pastor informed about needed directions, or it helps the bishop and cabinet identify gifts and graces needed for the next spiritual leader of the congregation. Clarity in consultation leads to the best possible match for clergy leadership.

There are times when pastoral change is necessary. Among the reasons for a change are a pastoral leader who has a new understanding of God's call, the appointment needs of the annual conference, and the needs of the local church. When this occurs, the S/PPRC conveys the local church's needs and desires to the district superintendent. The district superintendent utilizes knowledge of the local church's vision and mission to represent the church in the appointive process. Sometimes the local church and the bishop and cabinet will not agree. But, as a connectional church, experience has shown that the system works!

When an Appointment Changes

The staff/pastor-parish relations committee is the team in the local church that has primary responsibility for managing relationships when there are staff changes. In The United Methodist Church, ordained staff members are appointed to serve until the bishop reappoints them, and the appointment process is considered once a year. Each year (usually in January or February), the S/PPRC and the district superintendent consult about clergy leadership for the following year.

When there is a change in clergy leadership, some members of the congregation will be disappointed to see the former pastor leave. It is easy to become attached to a person who has been close to families in times of crisis and celebration. It is hard to say goodbye. When leaving, the pastor should express thanks for accomplishments and for having been able to help the congregation dream about the future.

SAYING GOODBYE TO CLERGY AND STAFF

The consultation process between the S/PPRC and district superintendent is confidential. (See comments in "Your First Meeting," page 15) Talk with the district superintendent about the appropriate time to request a change. Remember that the bishop makes the final appointment.

When the bishop announces an appointment change, plan opportunities to celebrate the ministry of the pastor and congregation during your life together. The S/PPRC can model for the congregation a healthy acceptance of and the process for grieving the loss of a pastor (and his or her family). Work through feelings of anger, hurt, loss, and fear of failure. Do not dump previous feelings and frustrations on the new pastor; let her or him begin with a clean slate.

Ask your district superintendent about a conference policy related to pastors returning to do weddings, funerals, or visitations. These life passages should be shared between the congregation and the new pastor, and it is a matter of clergy ethics and boundaries. The incumbent pastor is the proper person to invite a previous clergy or other staff person to return for pastoral functions. If there is any difficulty, appeal to the district superintendent for help.

The S/PPRC can provide opportunities for congregational members to write letters and make other expressions of appreciation to the exiting pastor. The *Book of Worship* has a service of farewell for a pastor.

People will be curious about the new pastor. The S/PPRC needs to be alert to avoiding gossip (as opposed to facts) about the incoming pastor. Use good listening and communication skills.

FIRST-TIME PASTORS

Some congregations will have the opportunity to be the first charge for a pastor. You can help the new pastor by setting two or three goals as priorities to help the pastor learn to allocate time. The S/PPRC needs to take the lead to check with the pastor on how well the goals are being met. Some congregations provide the first appointment for a series of pastors. These congregations may understand that their mission and ministry is to nurture effective pastors for a lifetime of service.

A NEW PASTOR IS COMING

The United Methodist Church has an open itinerancy system for providing pastoral leadership. From the beginning, when pastors traveled their circuits on horseback, our church has practiced this traveling ministry. The bishop and the cabinet work with the S/PPRC to appoint pastors. *We do not "call" them.* The bishop and cabinet examine the church and attempt to make a match, providing a pastor who has the skills and training to meet the needs and goals of the local church.

One of the reasons the appointive system works is the relationship that develops between the church and the district superintendent. A unique form of trust develops as the district superintendent comes to know the congregation—its needs, goals, and concerns. Trust develops when the S/PPRC has continuous, close consultation with the superintendent. Pastoral appointments are to be nondiscriminatory—made without regard to race, ethnic origin, gender, or age. The S/PPRC should discuss this openly with the congregation prior to a pastoral change and not wait until the midst of a change.

Sometimes the district superintendent is able to visit each church only once a year. Put the district superintendent on the mailing list for the parish newsletter, letters that go out to the membership, and even the Sunday bulletins. You may want to invite him or her to come to a meeting with the committee to share times of rejoicing at meeting goals or celebrating events such as anniversaries. Open lines of communication, again, are the key.

Remember that the work of the S/PPRC is confidential. Check with the district superintendent about when to announce the appointment of a new elder and deacon. Consideration must be given to the current leaders and to the other congregation where leaders are currently serving. *Remember that appointments are official only when the bishop announces them!*

Members of the S/PPRC should encourage the congregation to attend worship on the new pastor's first Sunday. The S/PPRC chair and committee introduce the new staff to the new community. In all sizes of communities, new pastors will have a quicker and smoother transition if they know who is influential in the community, the taboos in the community, community traditions and celebrations, community policies, and the practices and agencies available for social services. The S/PPRC tells the congregation and the community the pastor's preferences about civic involvement as well as the pastor's unique gifts for church and civic leadership.

Each pastor who goes to a new appointment may be grieving over leaving the prior one, and the new congregation needs to be aware of this. Pastors need time to get acquainted in the new community at large as well as with the congregation. Allot time for personal, spiritual, and family needs. It takes time for the congregation to discover the qualities of leadership that the new pastor brings.

Each time a pastor or other staff member begins a new appointment, a church has an opportunity for members to become personally involved in ministry. The gifts of all the people of God, lay and clergy, form the identity, the mission, and the ministry of the church. *Remember (and help others remember) that the pastor's family is not an extension of the pastor.* Share clear policies with the congregation and the pastor's family about the care of the parsonage (if there is one) and the privacy issues for the family living in the parsonage or elsewhere.

You should not be surprised if your new minister is a woman or a member of an ethnic group different from the majority of the congregation. Welcome this new minister to the congregation and community. The S/PPRC members need to be the leaders who call the congregation to hospitality and support of the new pastor. The S/PPRC is charged with setting the tone of acceptance, cooperation, and support of the new pastor—whatever the race, ethnicity, gender, or age. Affirm the gifts of the Holy Spirit given to all God's people and celebrate our oneness in God.

A NEW DEACON IS COMING

The heart of Christian ministry is Christ's ministry of outreaching love. The ordained deacon in full connection leads God's people in living daily in the community as Christian disciples. Deacons in full connection may have a primary appointment in your congregation and lead in equipping people for ministry through Christian education, music, parish nursing, professional counseling, administration, and other ministries. A deacon in full connection may work in the community and have a secondary appointment to your church. The S/PPRC has responsibility for all pastoral leaders appointed to the church, whether it is a primary or secondary appointment. Initiate conversations with both deacons and elders related to your church who have primary appointments beyond the congregation to learn about their ministry and to help the congregation understand how the congregation's ministry is extended through their work in the world.

The S/PPRC tells the congregation and the community about the ministry of the deacon. Affirm the gifts of the Holy Spirit in the ministry of the deacon. Celebrate opportunities for congregational service in the world and new forms of ministry to carry Christ's ministry of love and service to the world.

The ministry of deacons is described in Acts 6:1-7. When the church was thriving and growing, the disciples recognized the need for leaders to connect the body of Christ with the needs of the world. Read and reflect on this Scripture. Where does the community outside our church need to know the healing love of Jesus Christ? Who among us are living as deacons? What are similarities and differences between Christian service and civic clubs that do good works? Are there people in our congregation who should be encouraged to explore ordination as a deacon?

SECONDARY APPOINTMENT OF A DEACON

Increasingly, deacons are appointed by a bishop to an agency, a school, a social service provider, a health care setting, or some other setting where the deacon carries the love of the church into the world. These deacons have a primary appointment, salary support, and assessment outside the local church. Through ordination, they are accountable to a charge conference, which is called a secondary appointment. They relate to the S/PPRC at their secondary appointment. The S/PPRC interprets the ministry of the deacon to the congregation and mission of the congregation to the deacon. The S/PPRC assists the deacon to incorporate his or her skills and gifts to further the ministry of the congregation, while recognizing the deacon's primary appointment is outside the congregation.

Role of the S/PPRC With Nonappointed, Lay Staff

Churches of all sizes hire lay staff, full or part time, including musicians, educators, youth ministers, custodians, and secretaries. Churches are not exempt from federal laws related to hiring practices. Those federal laws are outlined by the General Board of Finance and Administration at http://www.gcfa.org/legalservices.htm.l Click the links to the Legal Manual and the Administrative and Judicial Procedures Handbook. You must comply with state and local laws as well. Guidance for legal and ethical practices is found in *Safe Sanctuaries,* listed in the Resources pages. All personnel records for lay employees must be kept in a safe, locked location and access to all records should be limited to people who "need to know." Check with a lawyer if you have questions.

As with appointed staff, there are many ways to support all of the staff. Build relationships with all people, getting to know one another. Assist the staff to build working relationships by encouraging them to take work breaks together, to celebrate special days together, and to learn new skills together. Help the congregation understand that they need to inform the staff when someone in the congregation is hospitalized or when someone needs a visit. Sometimes members feel hurt or slighted by the staff when the problem can be solved by better communication.

ANNUAL ASSESSMENT OF LAY STAFF
The S/PPRC is responsible for assessing the effectiveness of all staff and providing feedback for growth and development. The suggestions earlier in this guideline should be adapted for lay staff.

The S/PPRC can enhance the ministry of your congregation by alleviating stress on the pastor and the staff. Make sure your staff gets positive feedback, and monitor the quality of life of the pastor, staff members, and their families. Encourage them to have regular time off.

Specific Support
Annually review salary and non-salary support for every staff member. For lay staff members, assign a member of the committee to contact other churches in your vicinity to discover their salary scale for such services. This will help you determine equitable salary for all your staff. Other aspects of support for all employees are listed in this Guideline under the section on clergy "Financial Support and Benefits" (page 21).

For lay employees, give special attention to:

1. working conditions, including working space, procedures with office helpers (volunteers), equipment, and hours. Generally, background checks are required for all employees.
2. continuing education for all staff (time and costs). Remember to include continuing education for job skills, working together, and legal and ethical responsibilities.
3. benefits, including worker's compensation, insurance, pension payments, and social security.

Your committee's recommendations go to the finance committee. Their budget goes to the church council, though it may differ from your request. If so, the S/PPRC has the right and responsibility to advise the council or the charge conference of its recommendations and reasoning. However, the charge conference has the final decision on salary matters.

Personnel Committee of the S/PPRC

The S/PPRC should consider the need for a personnel committee. This is especially true if yours is a large church with several employees. The personnel committee would have the responsibility of recommending personnel policies, including hiring, supervising, firing, and financial compensation. Job descriptions, line of supervision, and job assessment would all be handled by the personnel committee, which would report to and seek approval from the S/PPRC. A very large church may have a staff person who oversees personnel and relates to S/PPRC.

> When hiring lay staff, remember to develop and post a job description, conduct background checks of candidates under serious consideration, contact references of applicants, and meet legal requirements. See Resources.

ESTABLISHING PERSONNEL POLICY

The *Book of Discipline* says that the committee and the pastor shall recommend to the church council in a written statement the policy and procedures regarding the process for hiring, evaluating, promoting, retiring, and dismissing staff personnel who are not subject to episcopal appointment (appointment by a bishop) as ordained clergy (¶258.2g[12]). All this must be done in consultation with the pastor-in-charge and with due process. A written personnel policy will help you and the committee through the maze of relationships that too frequently cause hard feelings that can last for many years.

These policies and procedures also need to comply with the laws of the state and any annual conference rules regarding employment by local churches. Check with your district superintendent or your conference staff for advice.

A CHECKLIST FOR POLICY AND PROCEDURES FOR HIRING LAY STAFF

_____ 1. Expectation of job descriptions
_____ 2. Recruiting, advertising process
_____ 3. Training qualifications and certification standards
_____ 4. Hiring (need for resume, references, background check, and interviews)
_____ 5. Statement regarding sexual harassment and misconduct
_____ 6. Evaluation procedures
_____ 7. Promotion procedures
_____ 8. Termination procedures
_____ 9. Grievance procedures
_____ 10. Affirmative action procedures
_____ 11. Health and life insurance
_____ 12. Pension benefits
_____ 13. Relationship between the employee, the supervisor, and the committee

When you have finished your statements, present them to the church council for approval. Provide copies prior to the meeting. Recommend that policies require action at two separate meetings before they take effect. There is help from the legal department of the General Council on Finance and Administration at http://www.gcfa.org/legalservices.html. You will find other helps at http://www.gbod.org/congregational. Click Articles and scroll down for items relating to personnel and policies.

Relating to the Congregation

the S/PPRC has the important task of communicating the work of the staff to the congregation and communicating feedback from the congregation to the staff. Annually, you will need to consider the following questions with the congregation, with other congregational leaders, and staff.

1. What are the goals of this congregation for ministry?
2. What is the neighborhood context where ministry takes place?
3. What is the job description and position of all the staff? How well is the job being done based on mutually understood criteria?
4. How can we help match our needs with the available skills? Will rewriting the job description help? Can the gifts of members of the congregation be used more effectively to supplement and enhance staff?
5. How can more members become team members to share the load?

Another role of the S/PPRC is responsibility to teach the congregation that all Christians are called to the ministry of a servant in the world to serve and witness with deeds and words that heal and free. (See the *Book of Discipline*, ¶¶120–36.) *Leadership for the church always comes from the laity. The heart of Christian ministry is Christ's ministry of outreaching love.* The S/PPRC can work with the lay leader and other committees to celebrate the ministry of all Christians and to help each Christian understand his or her role as a minister of Jesus Christ.

Candidates for Ministry

The S/PPRC is charged with the responsibility of discerning those whom God has called to represent Christ's ministry in the name of the church. This discernment is done with prayer and under guidance of the Holy Spirit. The S/PPRC has responsibility to recruit people who show evidence of God's claim upon them for ordination as deacons or elders. Persons interested in beginning a candidacy process for licensed or ordained ministry must meet certain membership requirements in the Church, apply to the district superintendent, register the candidacy, and work with an assigned mentor. (For details, see ¶311 in the *Discipline*.) Prior to being approved as a certified candidate by a district committee on ordained ministry, the S/PPRC examines candidates about their calls from God and the evidence of their gifts, and recommends these candidates to the charge conference. When the charge conference votes to recommend a candidate for ordained ministry, the congregation assumes care and support of the candidate through the years of preparation for ministry. The care and support may include continued prayer by individuals and during services of worship, cards and care packages during years of education, opportunities for worship leadership, financial support, and other forms of encouragement.

There is help for this task of recruitment in *The Christian as Minister* and the *Ministry Inquiry Process* (see Resources). At least one member of the S/PPRC should be trained as a guide for the Ministry Inquiry Process. The conference board of ministry provides this training.

Enlistment and recruitment of people for ministry is of paramount importance to the growth and development of the total church. Leadership that is Spirit-led and vision-driven helps the church to tell the good news of God through Jesus Christ. In this way, the S/PPRC ministers to and through the entire United Methodist Church, not only in the present but also for years to come.

S/PPRC Relates to Other Committees and the Community

Committees

Consult with committee chairs or administrators who relate to staff people (for example, trustees with the custodian; worship with musicians and worship leaders; education with the director of Christian education, director of youth ministries, and daycare teachers). These consultations will cover issues raised in the section "Support for the Clergy and Staff," page 21. As indicated earlier, your committee's recommendations for staff salaries and benefits go to the finance committee for its consideration.

The committee, S/PPRC, and staff should agree on what to report to the congregation and to the church council. Ask the pastor(s) and employed lay staff to evaluate the effectiveness of the S/PPRC work with staff committees. Review annually the responsibilities assigned and see what has worked, as well as what needs to be improved and ways that can be done.

Community

The S/PPRC can review with staff the need to lead ministry into the world outside the church. The community is where people live out their daily lives. In the community the lonely, the hurt, and the hungry, the powerful, the rich, the poor, and those in between are waiting to experience the transforming power of God's love. The church's mission in every age has involved developing disciples and sending them into their community, into the world. Raise questions with staff and lay volunteers about ways they equip the congregation for this ministry.

Recall too that many deacons are called first to a ministry in the community rather than to a specific local church. (See page 32.) Jesus models for us a ministry of reaching out to people with sensitivity to their needs and concerns, their hopes and dreams. Reaching out to the community and receiving people into the faith family means seeking out and accepting people just as they are. Seeking out and welcoming people who may be different from the current members of the congregation, or who may have different physical or spiritual needs, are at times frightening and difficult tasks. This is one of the greatest challenges for Christian disciples. The S/PPRC can help staff clarify the vision of the congregation for following the Great Commission. It is very important for the S/PPRC to support the staff when the congregation is challenged by the staff to reach out.

Resources

** Indicates our top picks

RESOURCES FOR PASTOR/STAFF PARISH RELATIONS COMMITTEE
- Holy Bible (there are many translations)

- *The Book of Discipline of The United Methodist Church* (Nashville: The United Methodist Publishing House, 2008 ISBN 987-0-687-64785-9).

UNDERSTANDING THE UNITED METHODIST CHURCH
- *The Organization of The United Methodist Church,* by Jack M. Tuell (Nashville: Abingdon, 2005. ISBN 978-0-687-33320-2).
- ***United Methodist Connections: What Every Leader Needs to Know,* by Linda Whited (Nashville: Discipleship Resources, 2004. ISBN 978-0-88177-436-8).
- •*The United Methodist Primer,* by Chester E. Custer (Nashville: Discipleship Resources, 2005. ISBN 978-0-88177-359-0).

JOB DESCRIPTIONS, STAFF ASSESSMENT, LEGAL AND ETHICAL RESPONSIBILITIES
- *General Board of Finance and Administration* Legal Manual includes policies and information on compensation, sexual misconduct, and numerous other legal and personnel issues. http://www.gcfa.org/legal services.html.

- *Guidelines for Developing Church Job Descriptions,* The General Board of Higher Education and Ministry. Free download from www.gbhem.org. Search the title.

- *Guidelines for Developing Church Personnel Policies,* The General Board of Higher Education and Ministry. Free download from www.gbhem.org. Search the title.

- *Guidelines for the Professional Staff-Pastor/Staff Relations Committee When Interviewing,* The General Board of Higher Education and Ministry. Free download from www.gbhem.org. Search the title.

- *The Ministry of Christian Education and Formation: A Practical Guide for Your Congregation* (Nashville: Discipleship Resources, 2003. ISBN 978-0-88177-395-8). See chapter 8, "Creating Job Descriptions."

• **Sample *church policy manual information,* The General Board of Discipleship, http://www.gbod.org/congregational/articles. Scroll down for related articles.

• *Safe Sanctuaries,* by Joy Thornburg Melton (Nashville: Discipleship Resources, 1998. ISBN 978-0-88177-220-3). Overview and help at http://www.gbod.org/ministries/family/safe/default.html

• **Watching Over One Another in Love: A Wesleyan Model for Ministry Assessment,* by Gwen Purushotham (Nashville: General Board of Higher Education and Ministry, 2007. ISBN 978-0-93816-293-3).

LEADING MEETINGS, PLANNING THE WORK

• *Behavioral Covenants in Congregations: A Handbook for Honoring Differences,* by Gilbert R. Rendle (Bethesda: Alban Institute, 1998. ISBN 978-1-56699-209-5).

• **Leading Meetings: What Every Leader Needs to Know,* by Betsey Heavner (Nashville: Discipleship Resources, 2004. ISBN 978-0-88177-433-7).

• *Spiritual Preparation for Christian Leadership,* by E. Glenn Hinson (Nashville: Upper Room Books, 1999. ISBN 978-0-8358-0888-0).

BUILDING SKILLS

• *Speaking Faith: The Essential Handbook for Religion Communicators* (Dallas: UMR Communications, ISBN 0-9679757-1-1). Go to http://www.religioncommunicators.org/handbook_7thed.html for an order form. No-nonsense information about every aspect of communications from developing a mission statement to choosing the appropriate media for a particular message.

CELEBRATION OF STAFF WORK

• *The United Methodist Book of Worship* (Nashville: Abingdon Press, 1992. ISBN 978-0-687-03572-4). See especially Section VII, "Occasional Services" and Section IX, "Services Relating to Congregations and Buildings."

IDENTIFYING MINISTERS IN THE CONGREGATION

• **Answering God's Call for Your Life: A Look at Christian Calls and Church Vocations,* by Robert Roth (Nashville: General Board of Higher Education and Ministry, 2006. ISBN 978-0-938162-94-0).

- *The Christian as Minister, Sixth Edition,* Robert Kohler and Sharon Rubey, editors (Nashville: Board of Higher Education and Ministry, 2006. ISBN 978-0-93816-298-8 through www.cokesbury.com).

- *First Steps to Ministry* (Video and Guide) (Nashville: Board of Higher Education and Ministry). Call 615-340-7389 to request these resources.

- *Ministry Inquiry Process* (Guidebook) (Nashville: Board of Higher Education and Ministry, 2008).

MEDIATION, RESOLVING PROBLEMS

- Articles, information on mediation centers and services, and congregational study "Engage Conflict Well" are available through http://www.justpeaceumc.org/.

- *Managing Transitions: Making the Most of Change,* by William Bridges (Cambridge, MA: Da Capo Press Publishing, 2003. ISBN 978-0-73820-824-4).